Dublin

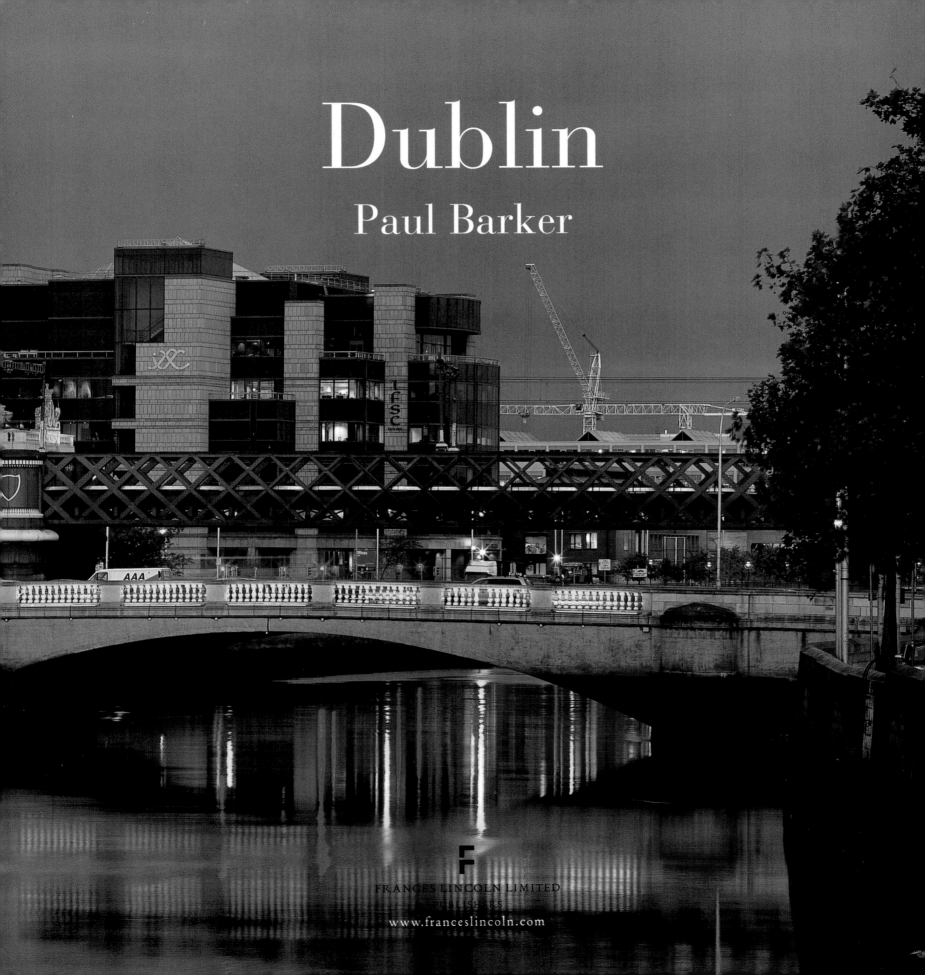

Dublin

Paul Barker

FRANCES LINCOLN LIMITED
PUBLISHERS
www.franceslincoln.com

Dedication

I would like to dedicate this book to Tracey and George with out whose help and understanding this book would not have been possible. I love them both.

Acknowledgements

I would like to thank the following people and organizations for their help during the making of this book

Desmond Guinness; Karen Kenny; Patrice Malloy; Deirdre Delaney; Elaine Walsh; Niall Bergin; William F. Roe; Ruth Ferguson; Father Pearse Walsh; Camilla McAleese; Ethel Hampshire; Michael Denton; Mary Forde; Edward McParland; Muriel McCarthy; Dean Robert MacCarthy; Anne-Marie Diffley; Angela Cassidy; Se Lenehan; Jacky Bryan; Anita McDonnell; Maria Malone; Sean McArdle; Office of Public Works; Dublin City Council; Tourist Office for Dublin; Irish Museum of Modern Art; Knights of Columbanus; The Honorable Society of King's Inns; Youth Work of Ireland; The Department of the Taoseach; The Department of Foreign Affairs; Country Life

I would also like to thank the people of Dublin for their hospitality and willingness to help, which is beyond compare.

Frances Lincoln Ltd
4 Torriano Mews
Torriano Avenue
London NW5 2RZ
www.franceslincoln.com

Dublin
Copyright © Frances Lincoln Ltd 2007
Photographs copyright © Paul Barker 2007
Text copyright © Paul Barker 2007

Designed by Ian Hunt

British Library Cataloguing in Publication Data
A catalogue record for this book is available from the British Library.

ISBN 978-0-7112-2745-3

TITLE PAGE
View looking east from O'Connell Bridge

Printed and bound in Singapore
9 8 7 6 5 4 3 2 1

contents

introduction

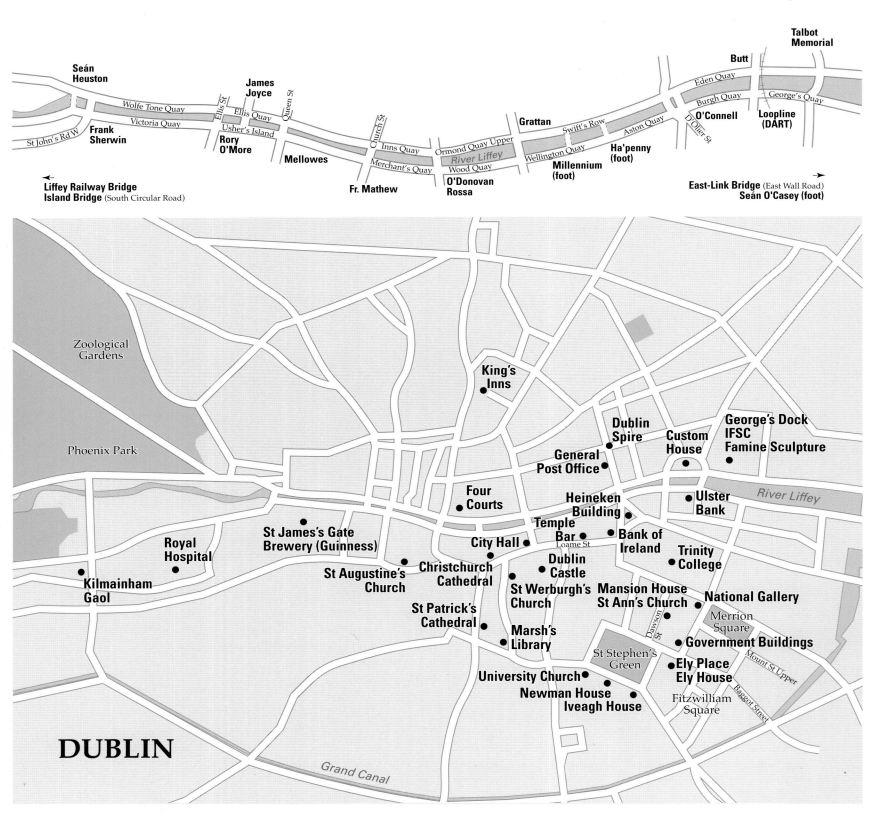

Liffey Bridges (top diagram)

Seán Heuston

Talbot Memorial

Butt

James Joyce

Queen St

Eden Quay

George's Quay

Wolfe Tone Quay

Ellis St

Burgh Quay

Ellis Quay

Victoria Quay

O'Connell

St John's Rd W

Loopline (DART)

Frank Sherwin

Usher's Island

Rory O'More

Church St

Grattan

Swift's Row

D'Olier St

Mellowes

Inns Quay

Ormond Quay Upper

Aston Quay

River Liffey

Wellington Quay

Ha'penny (foot)

Merchant's Quay

Wood Quay

Millennium (foot)

Fr. Mathew

O'Donovan Rossa

← Liffey Railway Bridge
Island Bridge (South Circular Road)

East-Link Bridge (East Wall Road) →
Seán O'Casey (foot)

DUBLIN (map)

Zoological Gardens

Phoenix Park

King's Inns

Dublin Spire

George's Dock
IFSC
Famine Sculpture

Custom House

General Post Office

River Liffey

Four Courts

Ulster Bank

Heineken Building

Temple Bar

Loame St

St James's Gate Brewery (Guinness)

Bank of Ireland

Royal Hospital

City Hall

Trinity College

Kilmainham Gaol

Christchurch Cathedral

Dublin Castle

St Augustine's Church

St Werburgh's Church

Mansion House
St Ann's Church

National Gallery

St Patrick's Cathedral

Merrion Square

Dawson St

Government Buildings

Mount St Upper

Marsh's Library

St Stephen's Green

Ely Place
Ely House

University Church

Fitzwilliam Square

Baggot Street

Newman House
Iveagh House

DUBLIN

Grand Canal

Dublin is today a vibrant and bustling city which never stops. The workers love to work there, the shoppers love to shop, and the tourists love to look. Dubliners are proud of their city and so they should be.

As you travel around today on one of the many open-topped buses and look around you can't help but notice as you sit and listen to the banter from the driver that in many ways Dublin has changed very little. Granted there have been many new additions since the 1990s and it is probably busier than it ever was before, but if you look beyond the crowds you can see that it is, essentially, very much as it was. Much of what you see in Dublin today is partly due to the poverty and neglect of the 19th century, when the lack of funds allowed the buildings

to remain untouched. There were changes, especially in the 1950s, when many houses were demolished. It was at this point that Georgian Dublin was nearly lost. One such example was in 1957 when Dublin Corporation decided to demolish half of Dominic Street; thankfully No. 20, a fine 1755 house by Robert West, managed to survive, complete with its fine plaster ceilings. Many more would have disappeared if it were not for the work of the Irish Georgian Society, founded in 1958 by the Honourable Desmond Guinness and his late wife Mariga; the aim of the Society was and still is to promote the conservation of distinguished examples of architecture and arts from the Georgian period, although the Society doesn't limit itself to that period alone.

ABOVE **Fitzwilliam Square South**

ABOVE **Baggot Street Lower**

9

Dublin is not a monumental city in the manner of London, Paris or Rome. But it does have some very fine buildings, such as the Custom House and the Four Courts on the banks or 'quays' of the River Liffey. Not far away are the King's Inns, the Bank of Ireland and Trinity College, all very imposing buildings, while Merrion Square, Fitzwilliam Square and St Stephen's Green offer a sense of space and grace. In Dublin they all sit very comfortably together, whereas in a larger city such architectural groupings may be scattered and lost.

ABOVE
Henrietta Street

OPPOSITE
Arran Quay and Mellowes
Bridge

history

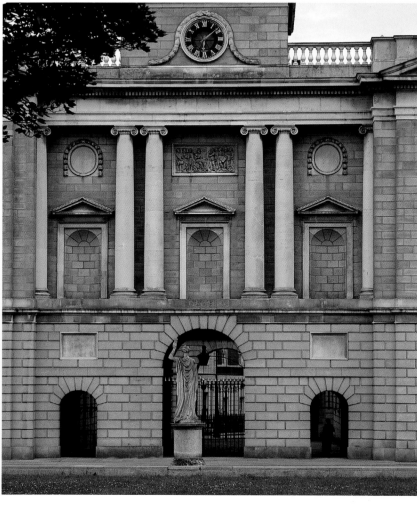

There is evidence of civilization in Dublin as early as 7500BC. Monumental tombs found in the Newgrange area, built by Neolithic farmers and herdsmen, date from around 4000BC. The Celts arrived in 700BC, with little evidence of any further changes until AD432, when St Patrick arrived in Ireland, bringing Christianity with him. The Celts were quick to embrace the new religion. During the age of Celtic Christianity the Dublin area had several churches. It is believed that the site of the present-day St Patrick's Cathedral is where the saint baptized converts around AD450. It was during these centuries that high levels of Christian scholarship developed, producing such treasures as the elaborately decorated 8th-century Book of Kells, now housed in the library at Trinity College.

Dublin's modern Gaelic name Báile Átha Cliath derives from a Celtic settlement on the north bank of the River Liffey, known then as Áth Cliathe, meaning 'the ford over the hurdles'. It was then the only crossing over the river, and it was here that bore the brunt of the island's first planned invasion by the Vikings.

In AD841 the Vikings established their first harbour in Dublin, but an alliance of Leinstermen drove them out in AD902. However, they returned seventeen years later in greater numbers, and built a stronghold located between the present Dublin Castle and Wood Quay at the point that the rivers Liffey and Poodle converged. The water at the confluence was still and dark, giving rise to the Viking name Dyflinn or Dubhlinn, meaning 'black pool'.

There then followed a period of feuding between the Celts and the Vikings which lasted for three centuries. At the Battle of Dublin in AD919 the Vikings fended off the King of Tara. In 1014 the Vikings were initially defeated at the Battle of Clontarf by the Irish High King, Brian Ború, who however perished in battle, leaving the aftermath inconclusive. Under the Viking King Sitric Silkbeard, whose continued reign lasted until 1038, Dublin became a Christian state, and he oversaw the construction of a wooden cathedral, later rebuilt as Christ Church.

The feuds between Vikings and Celts in Ireland continued into the early part of the 12th century, which led the King of Leinster, Dermot MacMurrough, to ask King Henry II of England to send an army to aid him. In 1169 Richard de Clare, better known as Strongbow, arrived, and within a year had taken control of Dublin and married MacMurrough's daughter. He also instigated the construction of Christ Church Cathedral. When MacMurrough died in 1171, Strongbow was in line to succeed him, but Henry II had other ideas and sent an army to Ireland to persuade him to retreat to his stronghold at Leinster. Henry spent four months in Dublin establishing control.

Under Anglo-Norman rule the city grew. Fortified walls and watchtowers were built, and in 1205 the construction of Dublin Castle was begun. St Patrick's underwent massive expansion and was made a Cathedral in 1213. By 1348 the city had become overcrowded and was struck by the horrifying plague known as the Black Death, which killed one-third of the population within three years.

In 1534 Thomas Fitzgerald, the ninth earl of Kildare, staged a revolt against London. This was easily defeated by King Henry VIII, who in 1541 passed the Act of Supremacy that made him King of Ireland and head of the Church. All land became the property of the English Crown; Henry dissolved the monasteries and sentenced to death all adult males of the Fitzgerald family. This began a strong-arm rule over Ireland accompanied by the forcible imposition of Protestantism as the state religion. During the reign of Elizabeth I, Ireland was developed as a British colony. In 1592 she made her mark in Dublin with the creation of Trinity College as a place of exclusively Protestant learning, an emphasis which was retained well into the 20th century. The site chosen for the new college was that of a dissolved monastery.

The grip over Ireland intensified in 1690 when the Catholic ex-King of England James II was defeated by the Dutch Protestant William, Prince of Orange, at the Battle of the Boyne, north of Dublin. Five years after his victory, as King

William III, he introduced the Penal Laws of 1695, the effect of which was to disenfranchise the some three-quarters of the Irish population who were Catholics in favour of the much smaller Church of Ireland. These laws were to have a dramatic effect on Irish history, right up to the sectarian conflicts which later plagued Northern Ireland.

Although William III's Penal Laws spelt hard times for the Catholic population in the rest of Ireland, Dublin's mainly Protestant middle class and aristocracy enjoyed a very comfortable existence. Throughout the 18th century the town grew enormously in size and wealth to become the second city of the British Empire. Many ostentatious homes, such as Leinster House, were built. The owners of the grand townhouses employed master craftsmen from around the world. Desirable addresses at the time were Henrietta Street, north of the river, and St Stephen's Green and Ely Place on the south side. The privileged Protestants were able to patronize the arts, Handel's *Messiah* was premiered in the Temple Bar area of the city in 1742. The Royal Dublin Society was founded in 1753 to promote the arts, science and agriculture. Many great academics emerged from Trinity College, including Edmund Burke, the philosopher, and Jonathan Swift, author of *Gulliver's Travels*, who became Dean of St Patrick's Cathedral. The Custom House in 1791 and the Four Courts in 1786–1802, both by James Gandon, are just two of Dublin's impressive buildings constructed during this period of Protestant Ascendancy. Commerce, too, helped shape the city: in 1759 Arthur Guinness opened his brewery, and in 1760 the Grand Canal was built.

Relaxation of the Penal Laws started in 1782, led by Henry Grattan, who passed a declaration of independence for the Irish Parliament and support for the emancipation of Catholics. The unsuccessful revolt which followed in 1798 convinced the government of England to impose the 1800 Act of Union, dissolving the Irish Parliament and introducing direct rule from England. The first 19th-century revolt against British rule was led by Robert Emmet, whose August 1803 attempt to seize Dublin Castle failed.

The rising degenerated into confusion and general rioting, but there were killings, some of which Emmet witnessed. This prompted him to call off the rising to avoid further bloodshed; he then fled into hiding. Emmet was captured in August and jailed in Kilmainham Gaol, tried for treason and executed in September of the same year. He was just 25 years old.

Daniel O'Connell was known for his more peaceful campaign for Catholic emancipation – that is, the opportunity for Irish Catholics to become Members of Parliament. As part of his campaign he stood for election to the House of Commons in 1828 and won. However he was unable to take his seat because of his refusal to take an oath to the King as head of the Church of England. The Prime Minister, the Duke of Wellington, and the Home Secretary, Sir Robert Peel, saw that denying O'Connell his seat could cause outrage and another rebellion. Although both Wellington and Peel were opposed to Catholic emancipation, the Act of Emancipation was passed in 1829. In 1841 O'Connell went on to become the first Catholic Mayor of Dublin. He died in 1847 at the age of 71 while on a pilgrimage to Rome. In appreciation of his work, his name has been honoured throughout the city. One of Dublin's main streets, previously known as Sackville Street, was renamed O'Connell Street in 1922, in which also stands the O'Connell Monument by John Henry Foley, built in 1882. The former Carlisle Bridge was also renamed after him in the same year.

The history of 19th-century Ireland is dominated by the Great Famine of 1845–8, caused by the total failure of the potato crop. Around one million people died from hunger

FAR LEFT
Essex Quay

LEFT
Boston College, St Stephen's Green

and disease. Many of them were poor rural peasants, eking out a living from tiny plots of land, who depended on the potato crop for their staple diet. Hunger to peasant families was not unknown, and there had been partial failures of the potato crop in previous years. However, these were not long-lasting and were confined to only a few counties. The Great Famine lasted a full three years and the crop failure affected the whole of Ireland.

The cause of the famine was a fungal disease which caused the potato plants to rot in the ground, giving off an appalling stench. The blight first affected America in 1842, followed by England in the summer of 1845 and then Ireland later the same year, first hitting the counties of Wexford and Waterford. Sir Robert Peel, the British Prime Minister, appointed a commission to investigate the problem, but scientists were unable to explain the disease, let alone find a remedy. In 1846 the potato crop was a total failure. Starvation was followed by disease: scurvy and dysentery flourished, and in 1849 cholera claimed many lives. Many sought to escape to America, only to drown at sea in overcrowded 'coffin ships'. Those that did make it arrived totally exhausted and at death's door.

By the end of 1849 the potato blight had passed and the crop eventually returned to normal, but during this tragic period the population had fallen by half, to four million. The famine was to prove a watershed in Anglo-Irish relations: the inadequacy of the measures taken by the British government left an enduring legacy of bitterness in Ireland.

New demands for independence from Britain were made and great strides began to be taken towards home rule. In 1902 Arthur Griffin founded the *Sinn Féin* newspaper, the name Gaelic for 'Ourselves Alone', and soon this gave rise to the political party of the same name. At this time of stark poverty

and violent clashes between workers and employers, political freedom became an increasingly important issue, and 1913 saw the formation of the Irish Volunteers (later to become the Irish Republican Army).

Although the Home Rule Bill eventually made its way through the British parliament, it was a long time coming. Its implementation was suspended due to the outbreak of the Great War in 1914. While Britain was at its most vulnerable, a small band of rebels felt that it was the best time to launch an attack on British rule. On Easter Monday 1916, Patrick Pearse and other members of the provisional government proclaimed the Declaration of Independence from the General Post Office in O'Connell Street. Under the leadership of Countess Constance Markievicz, the rebels occupied several buildings. The Easter Rising was over within six days, but its consequences would last much longer. Three hundred citizens were killed and much of the city was bombed. The British lost patience with the Irish cause and the main rebels were taken to Kilmainham Gaol and shot for treason. This was a terrible mistake: the overreaction by the British made the leaders into martyrs.

The years following were some of the bloodiest in Dublin's history. The resentment over the treatment of the Rising leaders, along with a British plan to bring conscription to Ireland, helped the cause of the Sinn Féin party, which went on to win three-quarters of the Irish seats in the 1918 election. These new MPs refused to take up their seats and instead met at the newly formed Dáil Éireann (Parliament of Ireland) at the Mansion House. The Dáil's Minister of Finance was Michael Collins, who was also the head of the Irish Volunteers' campaign of urban guerrilla warfare. Violence led to more violence, and on 21st November 1920 Collins ordered the assassination of fourteen undercover British officers in Dublin. The same

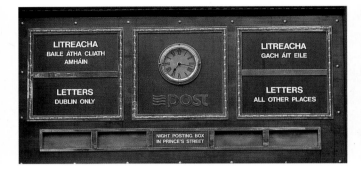

afternoon British forces retaliated in what was to become known as Bloody Sunday, when they sent armoured vehicles onto the pitch at Croke Park, opened fire and killed twelve spectators at a Gaelic football match. During the following months other skirmishes continued throughout the city, including the burning of the Custom House, a symbol of British authority, in May 1921. It was soon after this that both sides generally recognised that the situation in Ireland as it stood could not be allowed to continue.

In October 1921 Éamon de Valera sent Michael Collins to London to negotiate a treaty. The difficult negotiation lasted three months until a treaty was signed by Collins and Arthur Griffiths. This treaty gave only limited independence to what was called the Irish Free State. The six Ulster counties were excluded and members of the Free State Parliament (the Dáil) would have to swear allegiance to the British Crown. To Collins this was just the start of a process that would lead to full independence. However Collins was not truly happy and on signing the treaty is said to have commented, 'I tell you, I have just signed my death warrant'. There were many in the Dáil, including De Valera, who were bitterly opposed to the treaty and wanted a totally independent and united Ireland, and in June 1922 civil war broke out. Anti-Treaty forces occupied the Four Courts building which, along with O'Connell Street, was heavily bombed. The Free State government proved ruthless in its imprisonment and later execution of many anti-Treaty rebels. Collins himself became a victim when he was ambushed and shot in 1922 while on his way to meet the new Irish Army in County Cork. It is not known to this day what happened or who killed him. His body lay in state in Dublin for three days and thousands lined the streets for his funeral procession. In May 1923 De Valera ordered an end to the fighting and left Sinn

Féin. Within three years he had formed a new party, Fianna Fáil (meaning 'Warriors of Ireland'). By 1932 his party had acquired power after claiming the majority of votes. With only two short periods out of office De Valera held the post of Taoiseach (Prime Minister) until 1959, when he became president for a further fourteen years.

Ireland remained neutral during World War II and as a result Dublin experienced only one bombing raid from the German Luftwaffe. After the war Fianna Fáil were beaten in the election by Fine Gael, who went on to oversee the creation of the Republic of Ireland in 1949, which eventually severed all ties with Britain.

Dublin remained relatively immune from the long drawn out political emergency in Northern Ireland, although in 1966 the IRA bombed the huge Nelson's Pillar in O'Connell Street, the site of the present-day Dublin Spire, an adopted symbol of Dublin's future in the 21st century.

kilmainham gaol

Kilmainham Gaol was the most infamous prison in Ireland and many of the country's heroes were imprisoned here.

Built in 1796, the prison has a dark history linked with struggle, executions, torture and injustice. For the people of Dublin it was the most feared building in the city. The entrance was through a sinister doorway with its spy hatch, and the arch above entwined with five serpents cast in bronze, known as the Five Devils of Kilmainham. Above that was the gibbet where public hangings took place.

In 1857 the gaol was enlarged, making the main body of the building spacious and light, but the cells off it were small and cramped. It was in these cells where many of the rebels who fought for independence were held, before being moved to the cold, damp holding cells below prior to their execution. Robert Emmet was one, imprisoned in 1803 and later publicly hanged outside St Catherine's Church. During the Great Famine it was often the case that the desperate and usually honest commit-ted petty crime, just so they would be arrested and gaoled, knowing that they would at least receive regular food.

The leaders of the Easter Rising in 1916 were imprisoned here, and fourteen were executed in the stone-breakers' yard by firing squad before the sun had risen on the morning of May 3rd. De Valera avoided the death penalty because he was an American citizen. Today a small white cross marks the spot where those men fell, including James Connolly, who had been so badly injured during the fighting that he was unable to stand, and had to be strapped to a chair before being shot.

In 1924 the doors were shut for the last time. Ironically, Kilmainham's last prisoner was Éamon de Valera, who in 1923 was imprisoned here for a second time, before later going on to become the President of Ireland. Kilmainham Gaol remained abandoned until the 1960s, when it was decided to restore and preserve it as a shrine to those who suffered in the long and bit-ter struggle for Irish independence.

ABOVE
Kilmainham Gaol

docklands

The original port of Dublin was situated up river close to Christ Church Cathedral at Wood Quay. In medieval times Dublin shipped cattle hides to Britain and the continent, while the returning ships brought wine, pottery and other goods. Dublin Bay in its natural state presented many dangers for shipping: it was wild and exposed to wind from any direction.

In 1716 a bank was built to protect the south side at the mouth of the harbour. This provided only limited protection to shipping and after a particularly bad storm in 1753 it was replaced by a wall. Later a north wall was added, a measure recommended by Captain William Bligh, better known for his role on HMS Bounty.

BELOW
George's Quay and
Ulster Bank

Dublin prospered during the 18th century. Merchants shipped cargoes of linen and agricultural products to Britain and further afield, while the returning ships brought coal and luxury goods, much in demand in the great Georgian houses. By 1800 most of Dublin's trade was to British ports, as Dublin Bay was too shallow for larger vessels; most of this trade took place on the south side of the Liffey. Dublin's traditional industries of poplin and silk were located around the area of St Patrick's Cathedral. When these industries started to decline after 1800, the population in the older parts of the city fell and started to drift towards the Docklands. In the period between the construction of the Custom House in 1791 and of George's Dock in 1821 the port development shifted to the north bank, with its large warehouses and storage vaults. Up to this time the banks of the river were low-lying wastelands. As the port expanded down-river this land became more valuable. Until then, the only part of this area that had been developed was Ringsend – and the road from there to the city was regularly under water at high tide – but the land was gradually drained and reclaimed. Throughout the 19th century the population in the Docklands increased steadily and the area became increasingly built up with houses and commercial buildings.

By 1850 Docklands included two of Dublin's main railway terminals, along with hotels, warehouses, coal yards, cattle yards, and stables for the countless horses that transported goods throughout the city. Some of the larger employers, such as the railway companies, built houses for the workers, while speculative builders erected small cottages in the lanes and back streets to cater for the rapidly increasing population. It soon became a very highly populated area and not a very healthy one. Sewage was discharged directly into the River Liffey, while the gasworks and fertilizer plants emitted foul smells. The whole district had became one of Dublin's worst slums, including the once very elegant Georgian mansions

close to the Custom House where, for over a hundred years, thousands of cattle passed every day after a long drive, soiling the streets and generally causing chaos. The walk along the North Wall was the end of their long journey to the docks.

Working in Docklands was tough and injuries were common. There were often more men than jobs, and in order to get work it was not uncommon for dockers to resort to bribery. It was also a matter of who you knew, so it was necessary to live nearby. The work was generally irregular at the best of times, mainly because of the uncertainty of the weather. A fair wind might bring several ships and lots of work, while in more inclement weather the port would be empty and the dockers left standing idle.

Many other industries became established in Docklands. Coal merchants were scattered all along the quays, particularly south of the Liffey. Carters delivered the imported coal throughout the city. Glassworks established themselves at Ringsend, where again large quantities of coal were needed to fire the furnaces. There were several large flourmills as most of the wheat was imported, especially after the famine.

The houses in Docklands were often cheap and of low quality. By the 1930s they were in poor condition and beyond repair. Dublin Corporation and the Irish Government set about a programme of slum clearance, and they chose to re-house

OVERLEAF
View eastwards down the River Liffey towards Dublin Bay

LEFT
'Trinovate' Colchester at dock

RIGHT
Warehouse on City Quay

BELOW
North Wall Quay

families in the suburbs. From 1900 to 1980 the population in Docklands halved. Economic trends changed, adding further to the dereliction. The 1950s brought containerization and large roll-on, roll-off ferries, which meant there was no longer any need for large dockside storage areas. Sites became derelict and jobs disappeared.

On entry into the EEC in 1973 new industries were attracted to Ireland, many of them taking over from the more traditional ones. New factories were built, and the Port of Dublin became busy once again.

The Dublin Docklands in the 21st century is undergoing a massive process of regeneration, effectively extending the city centre down river with a mixed use of developments. There are huge development projects on both the north and south sides of the Liffey. They begin just after the Custom House with the International Financial Services Centre (IFSC), Dublin's business centre, where half the world's top 50 banks have offices. Within the new buildings of the IFSC are many regenerated buildings around George's Dock and Inner Dock.

The 'Famine' statues on Custom House Quay were presented to the city of Dublin in 1997. These extraordinarily haunting bronze statues commemorate the Great Famine of the mid-19th century and are the work of Dublin-born sculptor Rowan Gillespie.

Further on the North Wall lies the Spencer Dock development. On the south side there is the already completed George's Quay, while the major development of City Quay and the Grand Canal Dock area is ongoing.

In 2003 it was decided to go ahead with a huge twisting tower block on the south side of docklands. It is to be called the U2 Tower, and U2 are to have a recording studio on the top floor. The original plan was for it to be 60m high, but there are now plans for it go a further 40m higher, making it just 20m shorter than the Spire. This may have been the inspiration of U2's hit *Vertigo!*

the custom house

The original Custom House, built by Thomas Burgh in 1717, was sited up-river at Essex Quay on the south bank of the River Liffey, by Essex Bridge (now called the Grattan Bridge), at that time the last bridge before the open sea. However, plans to expand the city meant the building of a new bridge further down-river. This would have prevented the passage of any ships with tall masts, so a new Custom House was planned – an unpopular decision with city merchants who feared a move down-river would lessen the value of their properties in the city. A relatively unknown architect, James Gandon, was asked to undertake the building of a new Custom House.

The foundation stone was laid in 1781 on a site on the north bank, a mile (1.6km) further down river from the old Custom House. The building took ten years to complete at a cost of £200,000. The exterior of the building is richly adorned with sculptures and coats of arms by Thomas Banks, Agnostino Carlini and Edward Smyth.

In 1921 the building was set alight by the IRA and burned for five days. The vast majority of the interior was destroyed, but luckily the main body of the building survived. In the 1970s an extensive programme of restoration was undertaken by the Office of Public Works to bring the building back to its original grandeur.

the four courts

The Four Courts building derived its name from the four divisions that traditionally composed the judicial system in Ireland; these were Chancery, King's Bench, Exchequer and Common Pleas. Situated on the north bank of the Liffey, it majestically dominates the heart of the city. From the beginning of the 17th century the law courts had been situated on the south side of the river next to Christ Church Cathedral. In 1776 Thomas Cooley began work on a new Public Records Office on Inns Quay which was also to house the new King's Inns. In 1781 it was decided to build the law courts in the same place. In 1784 Cooley died, and two years later James Gandon took over. He already had the success of the Custom House behind him and he used many of the same craftsmen, including the Irish sculptor Edward Smyth, who executed the five statues on the central block.

The building was bombed during the Civil War in 1922, evidence of which can still be seen on the columns of the portico. The interior was completely lost, as was the Public Records Office and everything in it, including all the papers accumulated over centuries. Among them were parish records from all over Ireland and many important documents, maps and deeds from Christ Church and other historic buildings, priceless archives which ironically had originally been taken to the Four Courts as a place of safe keeping during times of trouble.

As with the Custom House a massive programme of restoration was needed, and by 1932 the building was back working, with a very different interior and each wing made twelve feet (3.7m) shorter to accommodate the widening of the roads along the quays.

RIGHT
**Four Courts from
O'Donovan Bridge**

king's inns

The King's Inns was established in 1541 when lawyers named their new society in honour of King Henry VIII. The Honourable Society of King's Inns now comprises benchers (all judges of the Supreme and High Courts), barristers and law students.

A lease was acquired on land at Inns Quay, then occupied by the Dominican Friary of St Saviour and today by the Four Courts. By the end of the 18th century the government decided that a new building was needed to house the dining hall, library and chambers, so in 1800 James Gandon was commissioned to design a new building at the top of Henrietta Street. It was Gandon's third building in Dublin and is often overlooked, being a little way out of the city. At the time he was 60 years of age and not in good health. He left much of the work to his pupil Aaron Baker, who some say should be entirely credited with it, although some of the drawings were jointly signed by Gandon and Baker. By the time the building was completed in 1817 Gandon had retired to his house in Lucan.

A tradition was established in the very early days of the society whereby students for the bar sat down to dinner with their peers in order to learn more of their profession, along with good manners. That tradition still exists today in the dining hall, which is the only major Gandon interior to have survived intact.

Gandon's plan placed the back of the hall and library at an angle to Henrietta Street, which had always been a cul-de-sac with open views at the top. The residents of the street – which contained the grandest houses on the north side of the city – were not pleased.

The magnificent doors on the main, west front facing Constitution Hill were carved by Edward Smyth, a man who had worked with Gandon on his two previous projects. The Triumphal Arch at the top of Henrietta Street boasts a royal coat of arms, the work of Edward Smyth's son John in 1820.

In 1822 it was decided to build a new library at the top of Henrietta Street. What had been the Lord Primate's house

OPPOSITE
King's Inns West Front

TOP
Entrance Hall to King's Inns

ABOVE
Dining Room, King's Inns

was demolished to make way for it. The new building was designed by Frederick Darley and work commenced in 1826. The library contains a very important collection of over 100,000 books, including those which formed the original collection, purchased in 1787. The cast-iron tables date from 1832 and were supplied by J&R Mallet of Dublin.

During a programme of restoration in 1997 the original wallpaper was discovered under several coats of paint in a ground-floor room. The 'faux bois' paper imitates oak with embellished borders. The paint was successfully removed and the room is now back to its original 1850s honey-coloured splendour.

henrietta street

Henrietta Street is one of Dublin's oldest and grandest streets, with the King's Inns situated at the head of the cul-de-sac. Building in the street commenced in 1720, so it is not typical of Dublin's Georgian streets, as most were built later. The houses are a on a grander scale than those elsewhere, some staggering in size, with a variety of doorway styles. The street became one of the most fashionable in the city, with archbishops, bishops and earls residing there.

The street was laid out by Luke Gardiner and included his own house at No. 10, now a convent. On the opposite side facing the convent is the King's Inns' Law Library, a granite-faced building which came late to Henrietta Street in 1827. This is at the top of the street, next to the arch and courtyard of the King's Inns, Gandon's last great public building.

The Act of Union in 1800 seemed to have a more devastating effect on the north side of the city than the south, and many of the houses degenerated into tenements. The survival of Henrietta Street is quite remarkable, probably due to the sheer strength of the original buildings, the quality of materials and the builders' competence. Today the street is probably the most evocative in the city.

OPPOSITE
**Under Treasurer's Office,
King's Inns**

ABOVE RIGHT AND RIGHT
Henrietta Street

BELOW
No. 13 Henrietta Street

OPPOSITE
No. 10 Henrietta Street

BELOW RIGHT
No. 9 Henrietta Street

38

dublin castle

In 1169 the Anglo-Normans landed in Co. Wexford and the following year, under Strongbow (Richard de Clare), captured Dublin, finally ending the almost 300-year Viking reign of Dublin. A few months later King Henry II arrived to ensure the new colony would remain under his control. A site was chosen for their citadel in the southeast of the Viking town, for the same reasons that the Vikings before them has selected it as their strongpoint – the eastern edge of an easily defended ridge at the confluence of two rivers, with access to Dublin harbour. The first Anglo-Norman fortification, which housed Henry's knights, was probably a motte-and-bailey type. In 1204 King John issued a mandate that a strongly built castle was to be constructed on the site to house his treasure and taxes, and also to establish the English base in Ireland. Progress was very slow, and it was not until 1230 that Dublin Castle, with its moat, drawbridge and portcullis, was completed. The defences were so strong that a keep was not necessary. In the often violent centuries which followed, the Castle served variously as the viceroy's residence, government offices, an arsenal, a barracks and a prison.

Then on 7th April 1684 a disastrous fire took hold, and within hours Dublin's medieval castle was ablaze. Several controlled explosions using gunpowder were carried out, with some success, in an attempt to stop the advance of the flames.

Even so, the castle was all but destroyed. In order to quell any rumours as to the cause of the fire, King Charles II issued a Royal Warrant which declared it had been started accidentally. Old walls and many towers had to be taken down as work started on the rebuilding. It was to be more like a palace than a castle, as the need for the fortified castle was over: the age of gunpowder and powerful cannon had seen to that.

By 1685 Sir William Robinson, architect of the Royal Hospital, Kilmainham, started work on the Upper Yard, later continued by Thomas Burgh. It was to take sixty years to complete. Today very little survives of the medieval castle apart from the lower walls of the Record Tower next to the Chapel. The centrepiece of the Castle is the Bedford Tower in the Upper Castle Yard. Built in 1761, it is one of Dublin's most magical buildings, with an extraordinary story to match. In 1907, just four days before the State visit of King Edward VII and Queen Alexandra, the crown jewels of Ireland were stolen from the strongroom inside. There were no obvious clues left by the thieves, both the front door and the door to the strongroom were left open, there was no sign of illegal entry and the safe opened in a regular manner. The jewels were never seen again. Many theories circulated as to who the culprit or culprits may have been, but mysteriously all papers relating to the theft have now been destroyed.

OPPOSITE
The Throne Room, Dublin Castle

ABOVE LEFT
Upper Castle Yard, Dublin Castle

ABOVE RIGHT
Dublin Castle

RIGHT
The State Drawing Room, Dublin Castle

trinity college

Trinity College, Dublin, is very highly respected as one of the great universities of the world. It was founded in 1592 by Queen Elizabeth I on the site of an Augustinian monastery, All Hallows. Originally a foundation for Protestants only, it began to admit Catholics under certain restrictions in 1793, but it was not until 1970 that Catholics were finally allowed entry without conditions. The university chapel is now the only church in Ireland to be shared by all denominations.

Of the early buildings very little survives, but there is a drawing from around 1600 which shows a red-brick quadrangle with hall and chapel. Another drawing shows that by 1681 the college had trebled in size. In 1689 great damage was inflicted on the college by the Catholic James II and his army as they marched into Dublin. It was forced to serve as a garrison for James' troops, and many of the chambers were used as a prison for Protestants. Nothing now remains of the Elizabethan foundations. The Rubics, a row of Queen Anne red-brick buildings on the east side of Library Square, comprises the oldest part, dating from 1700. The building of the great library commenced in 1712 to the design of Thomas Burgh on a site next to the Rubics. The lower part of the Long Room, measuring 64m (210ft) from end to end, remains as it was designed, although the original flat ceiling had to be sacrificed in 1860 in order to make more room for bookshelves, giving it the barrel-vaulted timber ceiling we see today. The Long Room is truly a wonder of Ireland, housing many rare and outstanding books, including the magnificent Book of Kells, which has been housed here since the 17th century. This world-famous manuscript book is believed to be the work of monks from Iona who in AD806 fled from the Vikings to Kells, near Newgrange. It contains the four Gospels in Latin and is richly embellished.

The Dining Hall was designed by Richard Castle in 1740, but problems with the construction meant it had to be rebuilt in 1760 by Hugh Darley. In 1752 work began on the main

BELOW LEFT
The Campanile, Trinity College

RIGHT
**The Campanile and Parliament
Square, Trinity College**

BELOW
Public Theatre, Trinity College

NIBUS MARMOREIS

west front by a relatively unknown architect called Theodore Jacobsen. In 1777 Sir William Chambers designed the Public Theatre or Examination Hall, and in 1798 he also designed the Chapel, which contains the original panelled stalls. An interesting point is that Chambers never came to Ireland, instead leaving a young architect called Christopher Myers to carry out his plans. All three buildings are beautifully situated around Parliament Square, a hub of activity, with students rushing between lectures, for the last 250 years.

The Campanile standing at the heart of the college in Library Square was designed by Sir Charles Lanyon in 1852 to house the two college bells. The Bell Tower designed by Richard Castle in 1740 had originally housed the bells, but was demolished in 1780 after having been pronounced unsafe.

The Museum Building, designed by John McCurdy from the firm of Deane and Woodward in 1853, is Italianate in style with carved stonework by the O'Shea brothers from Cork.

ABOVE AND LEFT
Trinity College Library

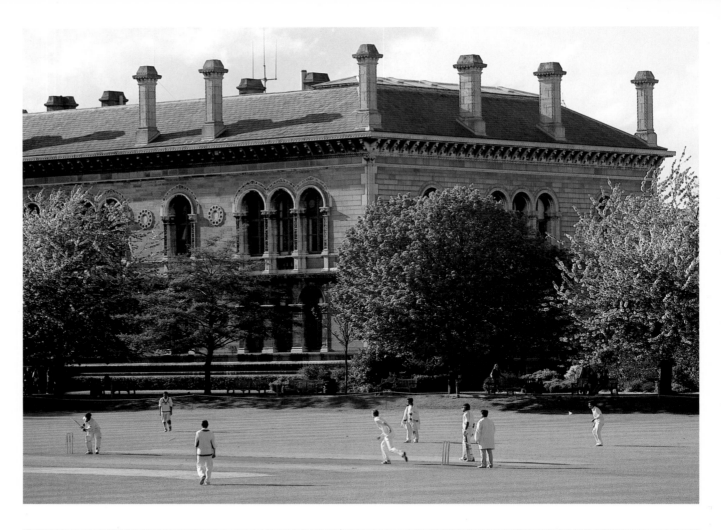

ABOVE RIGHT
Cricket match on College
Park, Trinity College

RIGHT
The Ussher Library,
Trinity College

48

the mansion house and dawson street

The Mansion House was built as a private house by Joshua Dawson in 1710. He had bought the land in 1705; two years later he had laid out the street which bears his name. The street runs north to south, with the Mansion House located at the south end. The house was sold to Dublin Corporation in 1715 and has served as the Mansion House ever since. It was originally a brick-built structure, but was radically altered in the 19th century, when the brick was rendered over, the windows altered and a cast-iron porch added. The rooms within are used throughout the year for countless official functions and receiving foreign dignitaries. Dawson Street was originally a tree-lined avenue with many fine houses. It remains a very fine street today, with St Ann's Church on the east side, along with The Royal Irish Academy. Kildare Street, running adjacent to Dawson Street, is another majestic thoroughfare, containing a number of fine buildings, none more so than Leinster House, which houses the Dáil and the Seanad, the two chambers of the Irish Parliament. The National Library and the National Gallery are also to be found here.

RIGHT
St Ann's Church,
Dawson Street

RIGHT
**Mansion House,
Dawson Street**

BELOW RIGHT
**National Museum of Ireland,
Kildare Street**

OPPOSITE, TOP LEFT
**La Stampa Hotel,
Dawson Street**

OPPOSITE, TOP RIGHT
**Sam Sara Café,
Dawson Street**

OPPOSITE, BOTTOM LEFT
**The Royal College of
Physicians of Ireland,
Dawson Street**

OPPOSITE, BOTTOM RIGHT
**St Ann's Church and Royal
Irish Academy, Dawson Street**

the bank of ireland

LEFT
Bank of Ireland and Trinity
College, College Green

BELOW
Bank of Ireland, east front and
College Green

OPPOSITE
Bank of Ireland, College Green

In the very heart of the city, the Ionic colonnaded south front of the Bank of Ireland, formerly known as Parliament House, stands in an unrivalled position overlooking College Green, along with its equally distinguished neighbour, Trinity College. The original building was designed by Sir Edward Lovett Pearce in 1729 to house the Irish Parliament. He was at the time Ireland's greatest architect, even though he was only 30 years old (and sadly only lived for a further four). His untimely death in 1733 prevented him from seeing his masterpiece completed. He was related to the great British architect Sir John Vanbrugh, and had been responsible for a number of other notable achievements, including Nos. 9 and 10 Henrietta Street.

In 1785 James Gandon added a Corinthian portico on the east front in Westmoreland Street in order to provide the House of Lords with its own separate entrance.

Parliament sat here for the last time on August 2nd 1800, when, under the Act of Union, Ireland was to be ruled from Westminster. Parliament House was subsequently used as an art gallery and, during the rebellion in 1803, as a military barracks. Soon after, it was purchased by the Bank of Ireland. Extensive alterations were carried out under the guidance of architect Francis Johnston.

OPPOSITE
Dame Street and Bank
of Ireland

BELOW
Ulster Bank, College Green

BELOW RIGHT
Bank of Ireland Arts Centre,
Foster Place

iveagh house and gardens

On the south side of St Stephen's Green stands Iveagh House, originally two separate houses. No. 80 was designed by Richard Cassels (Castle) in 1736, the earliest house in Dublin by the German-born architect. It was combined with No. 81 in 1863 when Sir Benjamin Guinness, Lord Mayor of Dublin and owner of the legendary brewery, bought both houses. None of the original front remains, as the two properties were subsequently linked together under a Portland stone façade. Extensive renovations were carried out at this time, resulting in the present mansion. Sir Benjamin died in 1868, leaving the house to his son Edward, the first Earl of Iveagh.

In 1939 the house was generously given to the Irish nation, officially accepted by Taoiseach Éamon de Valera, and renamed Iveagh House. Today it houses the Department of Foreign Affairs. The large ballroom at the back of the house is used for official banquets, while the original drawing-room of No. 81 is now the office of the Minister of Foreign Affairs.

Behind Iveagh House lies an almost secret garden, an oasis of tranquillity away from the hectic city life. Although it is open to the public, very few are aware of is existence. There are two very discreet entrances. Find them if you can.

BELOW LEFT
Iveagh House, Minister of Foreign Affairs' Anteroom

BELOW
Iveagh House, Minister of Foreign Affairs' Office

RIGHT
Iveagh House, St Stephen's Green

LEFT
Iveagh House, Staircase

ABOVE RIGHT
Iveagh Gardens

RIGHT
Iveagh Gardens

city hall

City Hall was built between 1769 and 1779 by the Guild of Merchants as the Royal Exchange. The architect was Thomas Cooley, the winner of a competition to design the new building. The runner-up was the perhaps better-known architect James Gandon. It stands at the top of Parliament Street, which was opened in 1762 as a convenient route from Dublin Castle to Essex Bridge (as it was then known), Grattan Bridge today.

The interior of the circular entrance hall, known as the Rotunda, is spectacular, with a spacious dome supported by twelve columns. This is where the merchants strolled and discussed business. The carved capitols are by Simon Vierpyl and the plasterwork by Charles Thorp. Trade was good at that time and the merchants wanted to provide themselves with elegant and spacious surroundings. After the Act of Union in 1800 the economy of Dublin suffered badly, and for forty years the Royal Exchange lay idle. In 1852 it was acquired by Dublin Corporation and renamed City Hall; the lord mayor and corporation have met in the Council Chamber here ever since.

The building has witnessed many dramatic events. It was used as a torture chamber during the 1798 rebellion, while the funerals of many leading patriots have been held here, including those of Charles Stewart Parnell and Jeremiah O'Donovan Rossa. It was used as a garrison during the Easter Rising of 1916, then in 1922 as the headquarters of the Irish Provisional Government under Michael Collins; later the same year his funeral, along with that of Arthur Griffith, took place here.

In 1998 the building underwent a period of restoration, during which time the Rotunda was opened up, with the removal of the 19th-century partitions, to reveal the original layout.

RIGHT AND OPPOSITE
City Hall

snapshots of dublin

LEFT
Ulster Bank, Dame Street

OPPOSITE
**St Teresa's Church,
Clarendon Street**

TOP Adelaide Road
ABOVE St Mark's Church

TOP Garda Station, Pearse Street
ABOVE Grand Canal, Mespil Road

TOP Baggot Street Lower. Reflection
ABOVE Scoil Chaitríona, Baggot Street Lower

TOP O₂ Building, City Quay
ABOVE Heineken Building

the river liffey

The River Liffey begins its 75-mile (120km) journey in Sally Gap near Kippure in the mountains of Wicklow. It meanders through the counties of Wicklow and Kildare, before gently flowing under the sixteen bridges of the city and out into Dublin Bay and the Irish Sea.

sean huston bridge
Designed by George Papworth in 1828, and originally called the King's Bridge. Renamed in 1941 after one of the executed leaders of the 1916 Easter Rising.

LEFT
View looking west from O'Connell Bridge

frank sherwin bridge
Built in 1981 and named after the Dublin politician.

rory o'more bridge
Built in 1859 and originally called the Victoria and Albert Bridge. Renamed in 1939 after one of the key figures in the Irish Rebellion of 1641.

james joyce bridge
Designed by the Spanish architect Santiago Calavatrava and opened in 2003. It is named after James Joyce, the quintessential Dublin author.

mellowes bridge
Built in 1763 by Charles Valency and originally named the Queen's Bridge. It was renamed in 1942 after Liam Mellowes, who was executed by firing squad during the Civil War in 1922. At more than 250 years old it is the most senior of all the Dublin city bridges.

father mathew bridge
Opened in 1818 and designed by George Knowles on the site believe to have been the first crossing of the Liffey. It was originally called the Whitworth Bridge, and was renamed in 1923 as Dublin Bridge, and renamed again in 1938 after Theobald Mathew, the temperance reformer.

o'donovan rossa bridge
Built in 1816 as the Richmond Bridge, and renamed in 1923 after Jeremiah O'Donovan Rossa, a key member of the campaign for Irish independence in the 1860s, who organized the first-ever bombings by Irish Republicans of English cities.

ABOVE
Arran Quay and St Paul's Church, Smithfield

LEFT
Arran Quay from Father Mathew Bridge

ABOVE AND LEFT
Ha'penny Bridge

ABOVE Ha'penny Bridge and Wellington Quay at dusk

ABOVE **Ha'penny Bridge and Aston Quay**

grattan bridge

Built in 1750 by George Semple and remodelled in 1872 after Westminster Bridge in London. Originally called Essex Bridge, it was renamed after Henry Grattan, who fought for the freedom of the Irish Parliament in the late 18th century.

millennium bridge

Built in Carlow, some fifty miles (80km) from Dublin, and transported to its present site. The span is a slender steel truss resting on reinforced concrete haunches. It was installed in November 1999.

ha'penny bridge

Built in 1816, it has had four different names. Originally it was called the Wellington Bridge, then the Liffey Bridge, followed by the Ha'penny Bridge, and finally, when the toll was increased, it was known as the Penny Ha'penny Bridge. This didn't last, and today Dublin's favourite bridge is affectionately known as the Ha'penny Bridge. The toll was dropped in 1919.

ABOVE LEFT
Ha'penny Bridge and Ormond Quay

LEFT
O'Connell Bridge

OPPOSITE
O'Connell Bridge and Bachelors Walk

o'connell bridge

Designed by James Gandon in 1794 and originally called the Carlisle Bridge. It was widened in 1879, and in 1882 it was renamed after Daniel O'Connell, the 19th-century politician who fought for the downtrodden Catholic population.

butt bridge

A reinforced concrete bridge, built in 1932, which replaced the original iron swivel bridge opened in 1879; both were named after Isaac Butt, leader of the Home Rule Movement.

loopline bridge

The railway bridge at Tara Street, serving the Dart line, was built in 1891 by J. Chaloner Smith. The construction is of iron girders and the bridge has, since its conception, been the subject of controversy, as it blocks the view of the Custom House. The debate continues to this day.

talbot memorial bridge

Completed in 1978 and named after Matt Talbot, a temperance campaigner, it is arguably Dublin's ugliest bridge.

OPPOSITE
Loopline Bridge and
Butt Bridge

BELOW
The Loopline Bridge and
Ulster Bank

OPPOSITE
Custom House Quay

RIGHT
**Sean O'Casey Bridge
and IFSC**

BELOW RIGHT
**Custom House and
Eden Quay with Liberty Hall**

sean o'casey bridge

Dublin's newest bridge, built in 2005 to the design of Cyril O'Neil. It is situated in the new Docklands Development, linking the newly rejuvenated north and south quays. It was named after the playwright, who lived in the North Wall area of the city.

east-link bridge

The last bridge before the river flows into Dublin Bay was opened in 1984 and is used extensively by lorries coming and going from the docks.

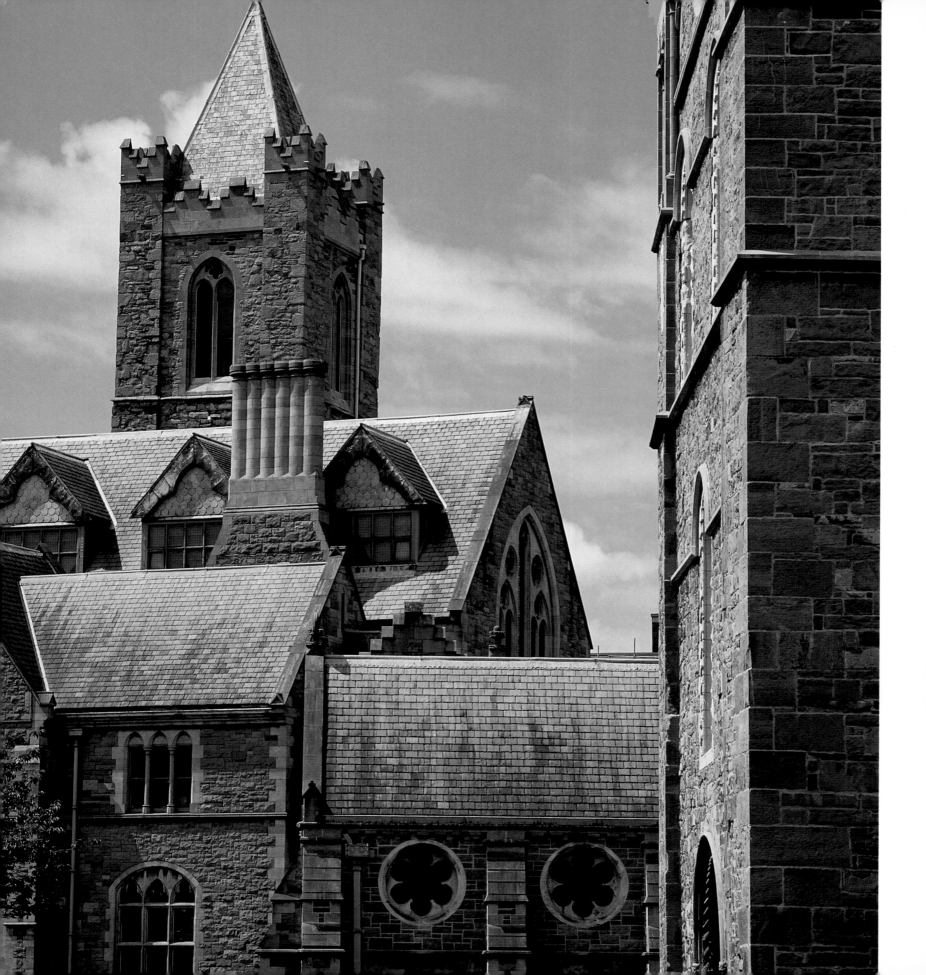

christ church cathedral

Christ Church Cathedral dates from 1038, when the Viking King of Ireland King Sitric Silkbeard built the first wooden church on a ridge overlooking the River Liffey. In 1172, following the invasion by the Anglo-Normans, led by Richard de Clare (known as Strongbow), the original simple foundation was extended and the cathedral rebuilt in what was probably an act of reconciliation. Strongbow died in 1178 and never saw it completed, but was nevertheless buried there. There were many problems during construction, none more so than that of the soil being too soft to carry the weight of such a great stone building. In order to overcome this, builders constructed stone vaulted arches to create the foundations, so giving it a crypt of massive proportions, extending under almost the entire cathedral, making it the biggest crypt in Britain and Ireland. Building was not finally completed until 1230.

By the middle of the 19th century the cathedral was in a poor condition and a huge programme of restoration followed, financed mainly by Henry Roe, a Dublin distiller. In 1871 George Edmund Street was chosen to do the work, with a brief to retain as much as possible the antiquity of the buildings. Street also designed the Synod Hall, incorporating the old St Michael's church tower, linking it to the cathedral with a bridge.

The nave seen today dates from different periods: Early English 1230–50, remains of the 1562 vault, and Street's 1870s restoration. It is lit by reproduction Georgian lights installed in 1999.

OPPOSITE
Synod Hall, Christ Church Cathedral

RIGHT
Christ Church Cathedral

st patrick's cathedral

Ireland's largest church was founded beside a sacred well where St Patrick is said to have baptized converts in AD 450. The original building was a simple wooden chapel and remained as such until 1192, when Archbishop John Cumyn rebuilt it in stone. In 1213 St Patrick's was elevated to Cathedral status, and the fabric was reconstructed between 1220 and 1254.

During Oliver Cromwell's sojourn in Dublin at the time of his conquest of Ireland, the Lord Protector stabled his horse in the nave. This was intended to demonstrate his disrespect for the Anglican Church.

From 1713 to 1745, Jonathan Swift was Dean of St Patrick's. He is best known for his work *Gulliver's Travels*, which contains a bitter satire on Anglo-Irish relations. It was possibly written as a protest against suffering caused in the area around St Patrick's – a maze of tiny crowded streets and a centre of the weaving industry – then hit by regulations imposed by England at the end of the previous century.

Major restoration work on the cathedral was carried out during the 1860s after a long period of desecration, compounded by fire and neglect. The restoration, financed by Sir Benjamin Guinness, took four years to complete. The work was carried out using drawings by R.C. Carpenter, made during an earlier restoration on the Lady Chapel. Although Sir Benjamin made many changes, the work was completed without an architect.

Dublin is in the unique position of having two Protestant cathedrals in the same diocese less than half a mile (0.8km) apart. There was always great rivalry between them, but this was resolved in 1872, when St Patrick's became a national cathedral for all the diocese of Ireland, while Christ Church was made the cathedral for the diocese of Dublin.

st werburgh's church

St Werburgh's Church, standing in the heart of the medieval city, near to Dublin Castle, was designed by Thomas Burgh in 1715. What lies behind the façade is quite difficult to appreciate from the exterior. Some believe that Alessandro Galilei, the architect of Castletown in County Kildare, may have helped with its design, which may explain its rather Italianate look. The interior, dating from 1759, contains some very fine decorative work, some huge memorials to the Guinness family, and a Gothic pulpit designed by Francis Johnston.

The main body of the church was destroyed by a fire in 1754, which however left the lower section of the Baroque façade intact. Today, the huge plain glass windows let in streams of sunlight, lighting up the dark wood of the highly carved pulpit, the work of Richard Stewart, and originally intended for the Chapel Royal.

There had originally been a spire on the tower but, after the uprising of 1798 and the rebellion of 1803, it was felt by the authorities to be too good a vantage point to overlook the Castle, and both spire and tower were removed.

st augustine and st john's church

Situated in Thomas Street, St Augustine's Church was commissioned in 1860. It was designed by Edward Welby Pugin and his partner and brother-in-law George Ashlin, in a style inspired by French architecture. It took nearly fifty years to complete and is probably the finest example of Gothic Revival in the city.

RIGHT

St Augustine and St John's Church, Thomas Street

newman house

OPPOSITE, CLOCKWISE
FROM TOP LEFT
Staircase at No. 86
Staircase Hall, No. 85
Saloon, No. 85
Apollo Room, No. 85

LEFT
Gerard Manley Hopkins'
Room, Newman House

The two townhouses at Nos. 85 and 86 on the south side of St Stephen's Green are of completely different styles and 30 years apart in date. Both houses have superb interiors with some of the best plasterwork in Dublin. No. 85 dates from 1738 and was designed by Richard Cassels (Castle). This is the smaller of the two houses, but contains the most beautiful rooms, with plasterwork by Paul and Philip Lafranchini; particularly outstanding is the Apollo Room, with the sun god above the mantel. The saloon, which takes up the entire first floor of No. 85, faces over the Green.

It was Richard Chapell Whaley, MP for County Wicklow, who in 1755 bought No. 85 and, while living there, began a much larger house next door, but died before its completion. Work on No. 86 started in 1765, with Robert West as the architect and stuccodore. He was responsible for the plasterwork

on the staircase, as he was also for the staircase at No. 20 Dominic Street.

The houses were joined together in 1853 to form what is now known as Newman House. The work was commissioned by the newly created Catholic University of Ireland, founded as an alternative to the Protestant Trinity College, and renamed after its first rector, John Henry Newman, who was later made a cardinal. In 1968 it became part of the University College, Dublin.

Former students at Newman House include Éamon de Valera and James Joyce. Today there are rooms furnished as they would have been when Joyce was a student (1898–1902). Another room is furnished in the style of the period during which the poet and Jesuit priest Gerard Manley Hopkins was a professor here (1844–1889).

university church,
st stephen's green

Dr John Henry Newman considered that a University Church would be an essential part of the new Catholic University of Ireland and, in order to achieve this, No. 87 St Stephen's Green was purchased. It was an ordinary brick townhouse built in 1765, but with a long garden, which would serve the purpose well. Building for the new church started in 1855. A friend of Newman's, John Hungerford Pollen, had been appointed Professor of Fine Arts at the University and was asked to work on the project. Although Pollen was architect, painter and decorator, the plan was Newman's; his idea was to build 'a large barn and decorate it in the style of a basilica with Irish marbles' (various colours of marble, coming from different regions in Ireland, line the walls). The entrance is of red brick, Byzantine in style, all very much against the trends of that time. The finished structure was very effective and Newman was delighted with it, although the building cost £6,000, twice the estimate. The extra was paid by Newman himself, putting him into debt.

ABOVE LEFT
University Church

ABOVE
University Church

OPPOSITE
Newman House and
University Church

the royal hospital, kilmainham

Built in 1680 by Sir William Robinson, two years prior to Wren's Chelsea Hospital in London, the Royal Hospital was styled on Les Invalides in Paris, and built to house 300 retired and wounded soldiers. It continued to be used for this purpose until its closure in 1927.

Since 1991, the Irish Museum of Modern Art has occupied the hospital's former residential quarters, giving quite an interesting mix of old and new, especially the modern glass staircase. Collections of Irish and international art are exhibited both in the galleries and in the grounds, including solo exhibitions such as the bronze *Hares* by sculptor Barry Flanagan.

OPPOSITE AND RIGHT
Royal Hospital Kilmainham

BELOW LEFT
Chapel Tower, Royal Hospital,
Kilmainham

BELOW RIGHT
Quadrangle with Art Exhibition.
Royal Hospital, Kilmainham

OPPOSITE
Royal Hospital, West Front,
Kilmainham

BELOW
Royal Hospital, Kilmainham
and a Barry Flanagan
"Hare" sculpture

OPPOSITE
The Irish Museum of Modern
Art, Royal Hospital Kilmainham

marsh's library

Marsh's Library is the oldest library in Ireland and is situated in part of what was then the garden of the Palace of Sepulchre, the residence of the Archbishop of Dublin. It was commissioned by Archbishop Narcissus Marsh and built in 1701 by Sir William Robinson, the architect also of the Royal Hospital, Kilmainham.

There are four main collections, consisting of 25,000 books in total relating to the 16th, 17th, and early 18th centuries. The most important collection is the 10,000-volume library belonging to Edward Stillingfleet, Bishop of Worcester, for which in 1705 Narcissus March paid £2,500.

Archbishop Marsh left all his books to the Library except his Oriental Collection, which he left to the Bodleian, in Oxford. Dr Elias Bouhereau, a Huguenot refugee who was the first librarian, also left his collection, while John Stearne, Bishop of Clogher, bequeathed his books to the Library in 1745. All the books are housed in the original dark-oak bookcases and also in the wired cages within which readers were locked to read the rarer volumes.

Today the Library is open most days, with Muriel McCarthy as the present Keeper.

Although many scholars and visitors go to the Library, very few are aware of the enclosed garden which has been part of it for over 300 years, and which was intended for the use of the first librarian, Dr Elias Bouhereau, a keen gardener. More recently the garden has been tended by Mary Pollard.

ABOVE
Marsh's Library,
St Patrick's Close

OPPOSITE
Garden at
Marsh's Library

merrion square

BELOW LEFT
Merrion Square South

BELOW
Merrion Square North.
Oscar Wilde lived here

OPPOSITE
Merrion Street South

Merrion Square is the city's finest and best-known Georgian square. The vistas of massive red-brick houses with their wrought-iron balconies, along with the variety of doorways and fanlights, make it uniquely Dublin. The square covers an area of some twelve acres (4.9ha) and was laid out around 1762 by John Ensor, who had been Richard Castle's assistant. The houses were usually built in groups of two or three, and it is possible to see the slight variations in style and, in certain lights, of the colours of the brick.

The north side was the first to be planned, with the work being carried out by a number of builders. The south side has houses that are more uniform in style and were completed in 1790. On the west side of the square are to be found the National Museum, the National Gallery and the garden of Leinster House.

Up to the Act of Union, the square was populated by members of parliament, peers and baronets. After 1880 this changed, and the square became home to the more professional classes. The square has had a number of famous names associated with it. Oscar Wilde lived at No. 1, Daniel O'Connell lived at No. 58. and W.B. Yeats, the poet, lived at No. 82. Today many of the houses are used as offices.

government buildings

In Merrion Street Upper, opposite a very fine row of Georgian houses (in one of which Duke of Wellington was born at No. 24), stands the very imposing Government Buildings. It was the last major project planned by the British in Dublin. The foundation stone was laid by King Edward VII and was opened in 1911 as the Royal College of Science. It was designed by Sir Aston Webb, the English architect who also designed the Edwardian façade of Buckingham Place. In 1922 the Irish Government moved into the north wing, with the rest of the building remaining a place of academia until 1989, when the RCS moved out to become part of University College Dublin. The Government then took over the rest of the building and a programme of restoration followed. Over eight decades, city grime had turned the Portland stone exterior grey, but this was now blasted away to reveal the building's original near-white appearance.

Today the building houses the Department of the Taoiseach (pronounced 'Tee-shuck') and Department of Finance, along with offices for other government ministers.

ABOVE AND RIGHT
Government Buildings

OPPOSITE
Government Buildings
(Going to work)

BELOW
Opposite the Government
Buildings in Merrion Street
Upper is the birthplace
of the Duke of Wellington

ely house

Ely Place is a very quiet cul-de-sac with several Georgian houses at the end of Merrion Street Upper. Most of the houses were built in the 1770s, around the same time as Merrion Square. It soon became a very fashionable and elegant place to live. The first to be built on the street was Ely House at No. 9, by Henry Loftus, the Earl of Ely. Constructed in red brick, it is located in the most desirable position, in the middle of Ely Place, looking down Hume Street towards St Stephen's

Green. Inside there is an ornate staircase telling the story of the Labours of Hercules. The dining-room contains plasterwork roundels linked by delicate ribbon decoration, the work of Michael Stapleton.

On the death of the Earl in 1783, Lady Ely continued to live there for a further forty years. There then followed a number of owners until the present occupiers, the Knights of St Columbanus, purchased the property in 1922.

ABOVE LEFT
Staircase at Ely House

ABOVE
Dining Room, Ely House

OPPOSITE
Ely House, Ely Place

OPPOSITE
No. 5 Ely Place

BELOW LEFT
No. 3 Ely Place

BELOW RIGHT
Ely Place

the guinness story

In 1759 Arthur Guinness signed a 9,000-year lease at an annual rent of £45 on premises at St James's Gate, so beginning a legend which continues to this very day. At that time the general standard of ale was not very good. In rural Ireland whiskey, gin and poteen were the much-favoured drinks. Guinness started brewing ale, but was very aware of the black beer, called porter, which was being produced and imported from London at that time. Porter was so called as it was very popular with the porters at Billingsgate and Covent Garden markets. Guinness started to work on his recipe for porter; he was so successful with it that within ten years he had made his first export shipment. Today the brewery covers 65 acres (26.34ha) on the original site at St James's Gate, and exports to more than 120 countries. The drink's distinctive flavour and colour comes from the roasted barley used in the brewing, and when the wind is in the right direction you can smell it all over Dublin.

A new development is the Guinness Storehouse, where visitors can witness the brewing process at first hand and see the historical development of the Guinness phenomenon – and, more importantly, enjoy a glass of the Guinness before you leave.

The drinking culture of Ireland is well known, and throughout Dublin scores of pubs and bars can be found, many with their traditional character unchanged over the years.

RIGHT
**Guinness Brewery at
St James's Gate**

BELOW LEFT
Doheny & Nesbitt interior

BELOW RIGHT
**Doheny and Nesbitt,
Baggot Street Lower**

RIGHT AND OPPOSITE
Hurrican's Pub

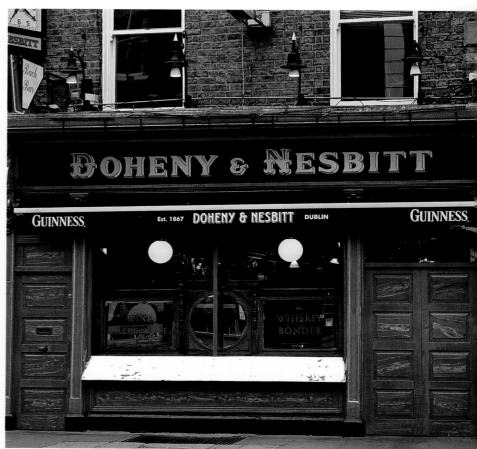

temple bar

The area of cobbled, narrow streets between Dame Street and the Liffey is known as Temple Bar, named after Sir William Temple, who acquired the land and lived there in the early 1600s. He was Provost of Trinity College from 1609 until his death in 1627. However there are other theories as to where the name came from, one of which is that it was simply named after Temple Bar in London, and another more intriguingly linking the area with the Knights Templar.

Most of the buildings in Temple Bar date from the early 18th century, the oldest of them probably those in Eustace Street and Furness Street. The area was at that time a flourishing centre of trade and commerce, with wine merchants, skilled craftsmen and artisans such as clockmakers and printers.

During the 19th century Temple Bar declined in popularity, and by the 20th century it was suffering badly from urban decay, with many of its buildings in a state of dereliction.

OPPOSITE
Eustace Street

BELOW RIGHT
Cope Street

Ironically, it may be that its very condition and unfashionability ultimately saved it from the property developers of the 1960s. In the 1980s there were plans to demolish the whole area and to build a bus terminus. However, during planning, the shops and warehouses were let out at low rents, which had the effect of attracting a lively mix of small shops, artists and galleries. This policy proved so popular that the bus station project was abandoned, and in 1991 the government set up Temple Bar Properties Ltd, a programme of regeneration for the area as Dublin's cultural quarter.

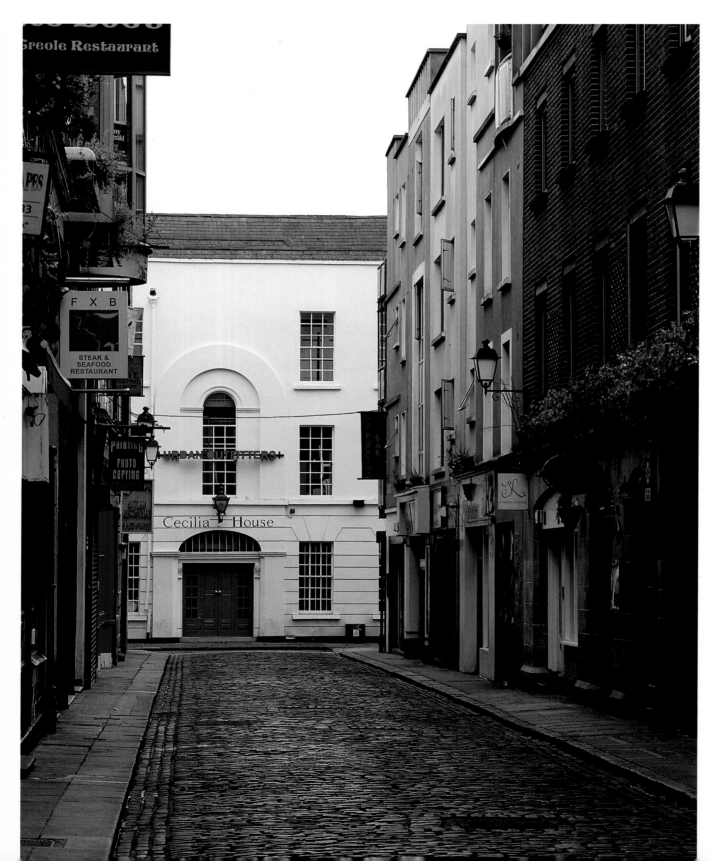

LEFT
Crow Street

OPPOSITE
Sycamore Street

Temple Bar today, with its unusual shops, restaurants and the best nightspots, is very exciting and atmospheric, a place everyone has to visit while in Dublin. Dublin's left bank also includes many Irish cultural institutions, including the National Photography Archive, the Irish Film Institute, the Contemporary Music Centre and the Temple Bar Gallery and Studios.

Temple Bar has preserved its medieval street pattern, and its many cobbled, narrow streets have managed to retain a charm that some parts of the city have lost.

ABOVE LEFT
Temple Lane South

ABOVE
Sycamore Street

LEFT
Essex Street East

OPPOSITE
Anglesea Street

eustace street

The ground floor of No. 25 Eustace Street was built around 1720. It forms an integral part of the streetscape of Temple Bar and it retains many original features, including the panelled interiors and staircase, very few of which still survive elsewhere in Dublin. The ground floor is occupied by the headquarters of the Irish Landmark Trust, a charitable trust which saves heritage buildings that have been abandoned. It restores and maintains them, then rents them out as holiday lets. The Irish Landmark Trust has a variety of properties, some in remote parts of the country and others, such as No. 25, in the city.

OPPOSITE AND RIGHT
No. 25 Eustace Street.
Irish Landmark Trust

the dublin spire

The Dublin Spire was designed by Ian Ritchie Architects, the winner of an architectural competition. It was erected in January 2003 in the middle of O'Connell Street, on the same site previously occupied by Nelson's Pillar since 1808, until it was blown up by the IRA in 1966. The impressive Spire stands 120m high and is by far the tallest structure in Dublin. It is 3m wide at its base, tapering to just 15cm at the top. The top section is perforated and lit by small blue LED lights. Its construction is of stainless steel, reflective in places and matt in others, giving extraordinary effects in different kinds of light at different times of the day. Today it is regarded by many as a symbol of modern Dublin.

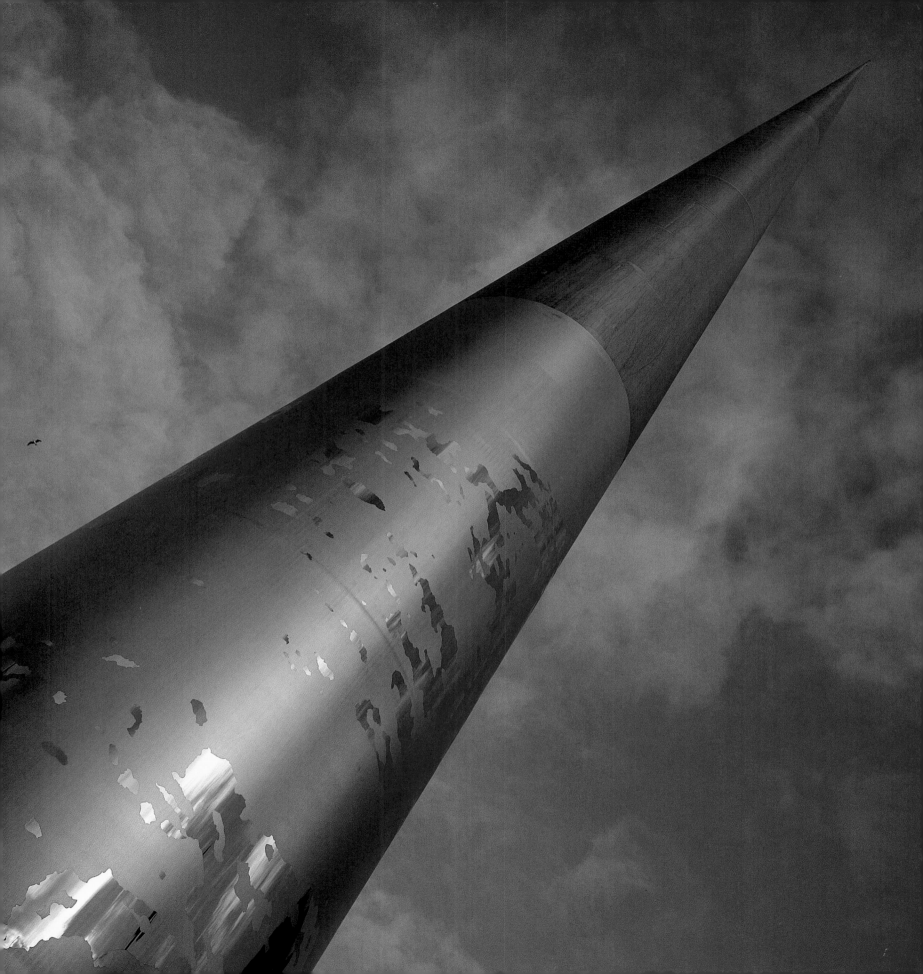

index